1

First published in January 2007 by:
Race Equality West Midlands,
iBIC, Unit 10, Holt Court South,
Jennens Road,
Aston Science Park,
Birmingham,
B7 4EJ,
UK

Tel: + 44 (0) 121 250 3859
Fax: + 44 (0) 121 250 3522
email: rewm@rewm.org.uk
website: www.rewm.org

© Frank Reeves
ISBN (10) 0-9552586-1-8
ISBN (13) 978-9552586-1-9

RACE EQUALITY IN LOCAL COMMUNITIES

A guide to its promotion

Contents

	Preface	5
1.	The scope of local race equality work	16
2.	Local race equality organisations and their functions	43
3.	Working for a local race equality organisation	76
4.	Race equality policy in social and historical context	113
5.	Developing race equality policy	150
6.	Urban race relations, community cohesion, and ethnic conflict	210
7.	Supporting communities and promoting good race relations	266
8.	Race equality law, human rights, and the Equality Act 2006	327
9.	Doing race equality casework	375
10.	Explaining race relations	409
	Discussion questions	463
	Abbreviations and acronyms	471
	References and bibliography	478
	Acknowledgements	504

3

Dedications   506

Index   508

Race equality practitioner series   526

Preface

For three successive years, Race Equality West Midlands (REWM) has arranged an induction programme for newly-recruited staff, trainees, members and volunteers of voluntary sector race equality organisations. As the news circulated, requests to attend were also received from staff from other bodies: Government Office, Primary Care Trusts, local authorities, and criminal justice agencies.

An umbrella body of the region's fourteen or so race equality councils, partnerships and kindred groupings, REWM has a brief to build race equality capacity by developing strategy, improving services, increasing funding, contributing to collaboration and communication, undertaking needs analysis and research, and offering relevant training programmes. The induction programmes, therefore, formed a key part of its core capacity-building activity.

What became obvious in preparing the induction programme was the vast range of topics competing for inclusion, the desire of participants to be kept abreast of the numerous developments in the field, and the unavailability of any single suitable background reader describing what local race equality practitioners actually did. Ready to hand was an assortment of government Green and White Papers, Acts, reports of inquiries, departmental strategies, policy guides, Commission for Racial Equality publications, research findings produced by different agencies including public authorities, various academic social science texts, legal compendia, newspaper and journal articles, novels, television programmes, films, and much else besides, all dealing with some vital aspect of race equality work. But none of these had been distilled to produce a set of essential topics, or a fundamental guide suitable for people wanting to participate in, or contribute to local work to promote race equality.

Since 1999, REWM has undertaken various appraisals of local race equality organisations (REOs) and their requirements, including two audits of the qualifications, knowledge, skills, experience, and learning needs of race equality staff. *The 2006 Audit of Organisational Capacity for Promoting Race Equality* (RED 20, July 2006) was targeted at managers, rather than at staff generally, but provided useful information about the administrative, human resource development, financial, strategic, project management, governance, information technology, service improvement, resource acquisition, and marketing skills available to voluntary sectors organisations promoting race equality.

The audits enabled REWM to build a picture of the qualifications of the staff working in REOs. Overall, two thirds were educated to first degree level. Of these, 85% of managers and race equality workers, and 30% of administrative staff, had a degree or equivalent qualification. *The 2006 Audit* showed nearly half of managers had master degrees or other post-graduate qualifications, many of them vocationally-oriented, for example, post-graduate certificate and diploma in management, and post-graduate diploma in careers guidance.

Any induction programme had to take into account the client group's overall educational level, motivating and inspiring its members by an appeal to their intelligence. To avoid the possibility of tedium, the content could not be confined to imparting common current practice and established organisational routine. It had to highlight, explain, evaluate, and justify the underlying theories of intervention on which established practices were based. And its method had to encourage maximal student participation through dialogue and debate.

All this accorded well with REWM's overall philosophy of questioning conventional interpretations of the world, prior to taking action to bring about change. At REWM, great store is placed on acquiring theoretical insight, developing critical distance between the practitioner and subject matter, and surveying and interpreting the field of action. It is important to establish whether the action taken is likely to achieve the intended result. The consequence of faulty diagnosis is that intervention, however well-meaning, may be utterly ineffectual, or worse, produce harmful side-effects.

Too often conference speakers have falsely claimed that time has been wasted on research, that there are too many data, and have urged practitioners to go out into the field and 'just do it!' Many historical battles may have been fought in this spontaneous way but none by the winning side. By way of contrast, this guide is based on the assumption that race equality is best promoted by combining the theoretical insights of social scientists with the practical know-how of experienced field workers. For far too long race equality interventions have been based on the assumption that the intuitive knowledge of practitioners is sufficient, and have fallen short of expectations as a consequence. Incidentally, conference speakers were probably right in drawing attention to the amount of data, but all data have to be critically interrogated to convert them into strategically-relevant information, and this process is frequently neglected.

The 2006 Audit highlighted respondents' preferences for training, programme content, and method. They expressed the wish to learn more about race and other equalities legislation, race equality strategy, demographic and social scientific background knowledge, and recent social policy development. Their preferred methods of learning were through attendance at seminars (83%), visits to other organisations and projects (62%), and through mentoring arrangements (55%) and case studies (55%). What emerged was the need for learning materials that dealt comprehensively but concisely with the aforementioned topics, and which could be used to support a series of seminars or, alternatively, for those not readily able to access such a programme, a scheme of distance learning.

The content of the resulting guide has been selected with these requirements in mind. But the topics covered, their order of presentation, and any related material have already been tested on those who attended the induction courses and owe much to their questions, criticisms, and comments. Their assistance in deciding on what knowledge is useful to race equality practitioners and what is not is gratefully acknowledged.

The final result can be judged from the guide's contents page. The local context in which race equality work takes place is first mapped out, followed by a full account of the voluntary organisations that undertake this work, and the common functions they perform. Their governance and funding arrangements are also explained. Who works for a race equality organisation and what is it like to work there? Examples are given of the tasks, roles, and responsibilities of race equality personnel and of how they are expected to work to organisational and personal work programmes. Nine critical success factors determine the survival of these important local agencies: these, too, are set out.

Chapters that follow alternate between providing the general background or contextual knowledge that explains why and how a particular race equality promotional function is undertaken, and offering a practical account of the day-to-day tasks relating to the performance of that function. Thus, the evolution of race equality policy, involving immigration control, anti-discrimination legislation, and area-based initiatives, is described in one chapter, followed in another by an account of the development of particular local policies aimed at eliminating institutional discrimination, and promoting equality of opportunity and good race relations. Similarly, a general introduction to urban race relations, community cohesion, and ethnic conflict, is succeeded by an exposition of the various community development projects mounted to encourage cohesion and resolve inter-ethnic group conflict and violence.

A summary of the way civil and criminal law regulate race relations precedes a more detailed exploration of the different kinds of information and advice given, and case-work and representation undertaken, by race equality organisations. The final chapter recounts how race equality is explained both in common-sense and social scientific terms, what narratives are preferred by race equality organisations, and the way they go about communicating with or educating others about the differences between racial and ethnic groups.

In all probability, however, the guide still includes a great deal of post-Second-World-War history and insufficient reference to the contemporary social issues besetting ethnic communities in the twenty-first century. The tendency to be heavy on history but light on present and future events is understandable, if not condonable, in a context in which the speed of social change is fast and its direction unpredictable. For example, while the pressure towards multi-strand equality work is obvious, it is still too early to predict the effect on race equality organisations (REOs) of the legislation to replace the Commission for Racial Equality (CRE) with the Commission for Equality and Human Rights (CEHR). The eventual outcome of government thinking on immigration, Islamic terrorism, multi-cultural policy, and community cohesion, is extremely difficult to forecast, as is its impact on REOs.

The guide presents the state of policy until Autumn 2006 and indicates possible directions of development. It is salutary however, to acknowledge how rapidly circumstances change, how soon current concerns become irrelevant, and how quickly the content of most books on contemporary social issues becomes outdated. To remain fully up-to-date and relevant, this manuscript would need annual revision. Without that revision, and given the pace of change in the field of race equality promotion, it has a maximum shelf life of about three years.

The guide is not a strategy or unitary set of proposals for promoting race equality in Britain. Neither is it a manifesto, emanating from a single agency, such as the CRE, or REWM, claiming a unique approach and solution to previously intractable problems. Rather it is conceived as a compendium of essential practical background knowledge gathered from a variety of historical and contemporary sources on how to operate in a local race equality organisation, much like *The Knowledge* is supposed to orientate London taxi drivers. What is offered, therefore, is a digest of key theories, perspectives, and facts about race equality, comments as to their success, and a selection of recommendations about future action. Although it can be read from front to back in linear fashion, the guide is designed to be entered and exited at any point with the help of paragraph headings and index.

The subject, of course, is immense and the task of deciding what to include or omit contestable. For example, the author is of the view that the circumstances surrounding the horrific death of Victoria Climbié afforded by the guide have important implications for race equality work, but some practitioners might disagree with the extensive coverage afforded by the guide of this incident.

The guide is not intended only to serve as a textbook and to provide background information for newly-recruited members, staff, trainees, and volunteers, working for race equality organisations. It also raises questions about the adequacy of contemporary race equality practice, and the need to examine goals afresh and develop new and more effective evidence-based strategies and techniques. Established race and diversity officers employed in the voluntary sector, as well as those working in public authorities and private agencies at local level, might benefit from studying this book. Potentially, it has an even wider readership. University sociology and social policy students interested in race relations, and in how they themselves might contribute to equality, human rights, and the reduction of conflict, might find it helpful. The wider public, too, may use it as a convenient and accessible reference to recent community policy and development affecting their local neighbourhoods, for example, the information on New Deal for Communities, Neighbourhood Renewal, and community safety.

The guide was produced in the three months, September to November 2006, and represents a large proportion of REWM's productive potential for that period, displacing other important elements of its work. Limited organisational capacity and tight deadlines may have adversely affected the quality of the product and, in particular, its accuracy. If readers detect mistakes, they are urged to contact REWM and point them out. Errata/ correction sheets will be issued if errors are significantly serious and have implications for practice. Otherwise, amendments will be made to any subsequent edition. Readers are asked to excuse typographical, grammatical, and incidental blunders that invariably occur in a manuscript of this length.

Much like a grain of coarse sand helps to grow an oyster pearl, editorial comment in a West Midlands evening newspaper, *Express and Star* (13.09.06), acted as an irritant to speed up the guide's production. A steering group in Wolverhampton had set up a new race equality partnership and placed an advertisement for its chief executive at a salary of £40,000 per year. Under the heading 'Do we need race equality councillors?', the *Express and Star* expressed the view that Wolverhampton had become a multicultural and racially-tolerant city, with no BNP councillors. 'For three years no one has even noticed that the Racial Equality Council isn't there'… There had been no sudden increase in race problems in the city. Race equality activity was useless, costly, unwanted, and unmissed, and City Council money set aside to support the new organisation could be better spent on other council services. 'The idea of people simply going about their business and getting on with their lives is an anathema to the Labour race industry. Instead it is looking to give some £40,000 a year for a non-job'.

The editorial comment showed a total ignorance of race equality work at local level and a failure to grasp what was going on a daily basis behind the scenes, with or without an REO, in order that the people of Wolverhampton continued to enjoy the benefits of racial tolerance and multicultural living. But suppose the editor of the *Express and Star* were to call REWM to request an account of what a local race equality organisation or its staff actually did? What response would be forthcoming? An accessible contemporary account of the wide-ranging work of race equality organisations, their objects, and their achievements simply does not exist, or REWM has not been able to locate one.

The guide to promoting race equality in local communities which follows this preface will not succeed in explaining to people the value of local race equality work in the face of deeply hostile attitudes. But, at least, it reveals the extent of the work undertaken in local communities to eliminate racial discrimination and promote equal opportunity and good race relations. What it probably does not do in sufficient measure is to demonstrate the degree of prejudice and discrimination, sometimes resulting in violent attack, that continues to blight the lives of minority ethnic groups and individuals in employment, residential accommodation, education, and other everyday situations. But were this to be the focus of the guide – which it is not – would it be sufficient to convince the *Express and Star* of the need for local racial equality work?

Incidentally, the main motivation of those who work in what the *Express and Star* calls 'the race relations industry,' certainly of those employed at REWM, is an acute awareness, arising from a regular experience of dealing with such cases, of racial discrimination, intimidation, harassment, criminal damage, and assault. Try telling those who have had excrement pushed through their letter box, windows smashed to a torrent of racial abuse, or children beaten up on the way to school, that they live in a multi-cultural and racially-tolerant society. Just talk to a professional black football player. Read the Macpherson report on the death of Stephen Lawrence. Editors who write that local race equality intervention is a waste of time and money, however, have an ulterior purpose and will not be persuaded by the weight of the evidence that follows.

Chapter One
The scope of local race equality work

> *Overview. Local race equality work aims to eliminate racial discrimination, and promote equality of opportunity and good race relations. It does so in a local context characterised by the immigration and settlement of people from other parts of the world attracted to the job opportunities and relative prosperity afforded by the changing British economy. The private, public, and voluntary sectors are each shown to make a distinctive contribution to local race equality work. Local Strategic Partnerships (LSPs) represent efforts to coordinate the contribution of the three sectors, to encourage joined-up working, to increase participation in local decision-making, and to promote race equality and community cohesion.*

What is race equality work?

Race equality work refers to action systematically undertaken:

- to rid society of racial discrimination, harassment and violence and to provide support for victims who are often, but not always, individuals from minority ethnic backgrounds, or recent immigrants.

- to create better opportunities for individuals and groups who are socially disadvantaged or discriminated against on grounds of colour, race, or ethnicity, in their places of residence, education, employment, housing, and other social contexts.

- to improve the relations between, and integration of people from different ethnic or racial backgrounds and, where there is evidence of conflict, to intervene and resolve it.

Continuing social change, continuing work

By any standard, work of this kind presents a vast and challenging task, more so when set in the context of uneven global economic development resulting in an accelerating movement of both capital and labour. What race equality workers are faced with are different communities, some more recently arrived, struggling to make a living for themselves in an already well-established competitive hierarchy of unequal social relations. When the question is asked 'have race relations improved over the last forty years, or are they the same or worse?', it may signify a failure to recognise that population movement, together with the social and ethnic relations it generates, is a continuous and dynamic process, alleviated or exaberated by economic and technical change and the expansion or contraction of the economy and labour market, either in Britain itself or world-wide. Race equality work is not like a steady up-hill journey to some tranquil retirement home, more a perpetual roller-coaster ride. Race equality workers are made redundant not because their goal of race equality has been achieved, but because the time-limited project funding for their posts has run out.

17

Legal framework

Race equality work at local level is still generally conceived and undertaken within the civil-law framework of the Race Relations Act 1976 (amended 2000). The Crime and Disorder Act 1998 created new offences, including racially-aggravated assault, criminal damage, harassment and provocation of violence, which has further expanded the scope of activity to that of providing support for victims of criminal racial harassment and violence, and of monitoring 'hot spots' of anti-social behaviour. The Race Relations Act makes it unlawful to discriminate on grounds of race, colour, nationality, ethnic origin, and national origin, in employment and training, in the provision of goods and services, and in undertaking public functions.

Institutional framework

Because the majority of the British population is committed to treating people fairly, irrespective of their race or skin colour, and this standpoint has the force of law behind it, various institutions have been set up, organisational arrangements made, policies put in place, and measures taken, to tackle unfairness.

Duties of the Commission for Racial Equality (CRE)

At national level, the Race Relations Act 1976 brought into being the Commission for Racial Equality (CRE) with the duties of working towards the elimination of racial discrimination, of promoting equality of opportunity and good relations between people of different racial groups and of keeping under review the way the Act itself was working. The CRE is the only body with a statutory duty to enforce the Race Relations Act, but its powers will be taken over by the Commission for Equality and Human Rights.

CRE goals

Currently, in 2006, the CRE describes its main goals as:

- encouraging greater integration and better relations between people from different ethnic groups.

- using its legal powers to help eradicate racial discrimination and harassment.

- working with government and public authorities to promote racial equality in public services.

- supporting local and regional organisations and employers in all sectors in their efforts to ensure equality of opportunity and good race relations.

- raising public awareness of racial discrimination and injustice and winning support for efforts to create a fairer and more equal society.

Public, private and voluntary sectors

As these goals show, the CRE works with and across the public, private, and voluntary and community sectors to eradicate discrimination and to ensure equality of opportunity and good race relations. The public sector consists of organisations, such as local councils, the police, primary care trusts and hospitals, schools and colleges, which are mostly funded from the public purse, and which commission and provide services for the general public. The private sector is made up of commercial and industrial businesses, such as British Telecom, or the corner shop, which sell goods and services and are normally run for a profit. Four fifths of the work force are employed in the private sector. The voluntary sector is composed of non-governmental and not-for-profit organisations, often charitable in intent, which contribute to the quality and richness of life by, for example, alleviating the effects of poverty, assisting the elderly, sick, infirm, vulnerable, or victims of injustice, or promoting culture, sport, recreation, or the arts. Examples are Oxfam, Age Concern, and the Citizens Advice Bureaux. The title 'voluntary' is misleading because, while a great deal of volunteering goes on, many staff in the voluntary sector are paid. The 'voluntary' is meant to contrast to 'statutory' bodies legislated into being by the government.

Sectors' compliance with race relations legislation

Each of the sectors described above must comply with race relations legislation when providing employment, training, goods and services. In addition, following amendments to the Race Relations Act in

2000, listed public authorities in the public sector have an extra statutory duty to promote race equality positively. If they fail to do so, the CRE can serve a compliance notice on them which is enforceable through the County Court. The public, private, and voluntary and community sectors have responded in different ways to social, economic and legal pressures to eliminate racial discrimination, promote equality of opportunity, and foster good race relations.

The public sector

Public sector agencies, such as local councils, often employ thousands of people and commission, or themselves provide, a wide range of public services. Major public services include education, health, environmental services, social housing, some public transport, the police and other criminal justice agencies. Many of these bodies have for some time implemented race equality policies and monitored ethnically their employees and user uptake of their services, for example, social housing tenancies. The original aim was to ensure there were no discriminatory barriers to accessing these facilities.

The Race Relations (Amendment) Act 2000

In addition, the Race Relations (Amendment) Act 2000 requires public authorities to promote race equality in relation to their policy, service delivery, and employment practices. Listed authorities must undertake general and specific duties (see Chapter Five). These usually require an authority to produce a race equality scheme or policy, part of which involves undertaking a comprehensive review of its functions, policies and proposals.

Specialist diversity units

When public authorities first embarked on this course of action, they sought expert advice from external agencies but, as time went on, they appointed their own equality staff. The larger agencies now have specialist units, free-standing, or attached to, for example, a chief executive's or human resource department, to ensure they comply with race relations and other equalities legislation, improve the suitability for different user groups of their services, and perform well in terms of best value and other performance indicators (including indicators relating to race and other equalities).

Service improvement agenda

The promotion of race equality in the public sector is frequently treated as an integral part of the government's efforts to improve public services and raise service standards, thus contributing to equality by making available collective social benefits. The imposition on public authorities of the statutory race equality duty is often interpreted by them as a further means of upgrading their services. In 2004, the Audit Commission produced a report on delivering improved services to local communities. The report found that people of black and minority ethnic origin were more likely to be dissatisfied with public services than whites, and public services more likely to fall short of expectations, although the reasons for differences in satisfaction between groups were complex. The Audit Commission argues that services would be improved overall if the concerns of minority ethnic communities were addressed. Outcomes contributing to improving the quality of life for minority ethnic communities were: influence over decision-making, better access to services and information, more employment opportunities, and increased trust (for more detail see Chapter Five).

Generic equalities approach

The public sector has gradually rationalised its approach to the various strands of equality – especially in regard to race, gender, and disability – and now works mostly to a generic equal opportunity policy when dealing with employment and training, service delivery, and other functions. Many of the larger public authorities have a team of specialist equality and diversity officers to ensure that the organisation is in compliance with the law, produces and works to agreed equality schemes and standards, and is improving the life chances of all service users in the overall drive for public sector service improvement.

Race equality and the public sector

In short, public authorities:

- have had in place for some time equal opportunity policies aimed at ensuring they do not discriminate racially in employment or service provision.

- must 'have due regard' to the need to eliminate unlawful racial discrimination, and promote equality of opportunity and good relations between people of different racial groups. Many are also required to have a race equality scheme, that is, a timetabled and realistic plan setting out arrangements for promoting race equality.

- often have specialist staff in place pursuing a generic equalities policy, to ensure the organisation complies with the requirements of the laws relating to equality.

- vary considerably in their success in recruiting minority ethnic staff, providing services relevant and sensitive to ethnic groups' needs, eliminating 'institutional racism', achieving equality standard levels, and meeting race equality targets.

- sometimes pursue active overseas recruitment to fill labour shortages in what has been until recently a comparatively poorly-paid sector.

The private sector

The private sector provides goods and services for profit and tends to judge its success on sales figures rather than on separate indices of user satisfaction. The service improvement model of race equality promotion cannot easily or successfully be applied to the operation of private companies. They are not bound by any general duty to promote race equality as in the public sector but they most comply with the anti-discrimination clauses of the Race Relations Act.

Diversity management

Some firms, instead, have chosen to adopt a policy of 'managing diversity' (see Chapter Five), which involves them trying to capitalise on the fact that their workforce, actual or potential, comprises people from many different backgrounds, with a wide range of skills and experiences. By embracing so-called ethnic and cultural (as well as gender and age) diversity, managers are able to identify extra sources of labour, tap skills and experience, release creative energy, and enter new markets. Diversity management and diversity mangers aim to improve the effectiveness with which companies make use of the full range of human resources at their disposal and thus contribute to their profitability.

Compliance with race relations law

Most importantly, however, organisations in the private sector must ensure that they do not run foul of race relations legislation and find themselves accused of discrimination in an Employment Tribunal or County Court. They might, as a consequence, have to pay legal bills and compensation and incur adverse publicity. When firms have run into trouble in this way, they sometimes employ private consultants, usually in the field of human resource management, to overhaul their policies and procedures. The private sector has usually sought private sector solutions to its race relations problems.

Race equality and the private sector

In short, organisations in the private sector:

- wish to avoid the costs of not complying with equality legislation.

- do not want their customers to complain about poor or inappropriate services, nor to receive adverse publicity relating to their treatment of ethnic individuals or groups.

- sometimes recognise the added value of adopting proactive diversity management strategies.

- collectively create the demand for labour and seek to secure the supply of labour, which can result in new immigration.

- are generally opposed to any action, such as rioting in urban settings, that may damage or disrupt normal commercial activity.

The voluntary and community sector

Sector diversity

The voluntary and community sector is somewhat of a catch-all label. The sector is often subdivided into smaller categories, such as advice and counselling agencies, direct assisters (Help the Aged), educational, not-for-profit providers (e.g. housing associations), political pressure, religious and faith, self help, community, and black and minority ethnic groups. It is estimated that there are some 400,000 voluntary and community organisations in the UK of which about two fifths are registered charities. They vary greatly in size. The giants such as Oxfam and Banardo's have an annual income in excess of £100 million but the vast majority are small with an income of less than £10,000 per year. Sometimes a sub-division of the voluntary and community sector as a whole consisting of voluntary organisations is contrasted with a sub-division made up of community groups. An argument has also been made for a separate political sector consisting of political parties, trade unions and other pressure groups which, while 'voluntary', and 'not for profit', has distinctive political objectives. Charles Handy (1988) divides voluntary activity into three broad types: mutual support, service delivery, and campaigning. In the field of race and ethnic relations, a category of black and minority ethnic (community) groups is often distinguished.

Race equality in local communities

Responding to community need

The voluntary and community sector, almost by definition, is a direct product and expression of the daily needs, concerns and activities of communities of geography and interest. It can be seen as responding to and satisfying social requirements that initially remain unrecognised and unmet either by private sector market forces or public sector service provision. It is often driven by socially committed people who give freely of their time. In regard to race equality promotion, Councils for Racial Harmony and Community Relations Councils, forerunners of today's Racial Equality Councils and Partnerships, were originally set up to provide practical help and a campaigning voice for New Commonwealth immigrants who came with their families to work in Britain in the twenty-five-year period after the Second World War (see Chapter Four).

Responding to New Commonwealth immigration

There was widespread and covert racial discrimination at the time in housing, employment, service provision and recreational facilities, and no effective legislation to prohibit it. Supported by sympathetic whites and associations of recently-arrived black and minority ethnic immigrants, the 'councils' provided (i) a united front in the face of hostility from right-wing nationalism and the remaining imperial delusions of white supremacy, (ii) mutual support especially for local black and minority ethnic residents and (iii) most importantly, a campaigning voice for racial justice, human rights, respect, and equality of treatment, for example, by the police, social housing officers, or school teachers.

Creating the institutional framework

Responding to the case made for legislation, the government passed increasingly comprehensive Race Relations Acts in 1965, 1968, and 1976. Voluntary action by MPs, progressive forces, and black and minority ethnic groups, led to the setting up of new national statutory government-funded bodies such as the National Committee for Commonwealth Immigrants and the Race Relations Board (1965), the Community Relations Commission (1968) and, eventually, the Commission for Racial Equality (1976). These bodies, in turn, determined the context in which the voluntary sector developed and operated.

The range of voluntary and community sector responses

Race equality councils and partnerships are the direct successors of early local voluntary initiatives, but the voluntary sector has spontaneously spawned a whole range of responses to minority ethnic needs and to the process and effects of continued inward migration and settlement. The following bullets attempt to summarise these activities:

- General race equality promotion: community development, policy development, complainant-aid provision, and public awareness-raising by race equality councils and partnerships.

- Specialist social welfare provision for black and minority ethnic individuals and groups provided by, for example, Caribbean housing associations, Asian day centres, sickle cell and thalasemia support groups.

- Specific black and minority ethnic cultural, community and recreational activities, often organised around 'cultural centres'.

- Black and minority ethnic religious activities and projects centred on places of worship.

- Expatriot groups' political campaigning.

- Immigrant and refugee support.

- Black and minority ethnic voluntary sector 'umbrella' networking, frequently committed to capacity-building affiliated organisations.

- Mainstream voluntary agency project work targeted at black and minority ethnic individuals and groups.

- Human rights campaigning.

- Legal advice.

The scope of local race equality work

Race equality councils versus black and minority ethnic self-help

Not surprisingly, with the formation of black and minority ethnic groups aiming to promote their individual community interest, the question was soon raised as to whether race equality councils, created in the early years to promote black and minority ethnic collective interest in the face of discrimination by white institutions, political groups and individuals, had outlived their usefulness. Were the race equality councils simply a sophisticated way of controlling ethnic minority communities or mediating between them and entrenched authority (sometimes abusively described as 'administering Bantu affairs')?

The urban/rural dimension

In urban areas, with developed minority ethnic pressure groups, race equality councils which sought to speak on behalf of ethnic communities might well have deserved this criticism, but in county towns and rural areas, where the black and minority ethnic presence was thin on the ground, there was still very good reason for retaining a collective voice.

Countering community fragmentation

After the northern riots in 2001 and their analysis in terms of 'community fragmentation' and 'parallel lives' the distinction between the 'bridging' and 'bringing together' functions of the race equality councils on the one hand, and the pursuit of an individual ethnic group's self-interest on the other, became much more apparent. The need for an

Race equality in local communities

organisation that specifically and impartially promoted race equality and good race relations was once more publicly reaffirmed.

Race equality and the voluntary and community sector

In summary, the voluntary and community sector:

- is conceived as recognising the emerging needs of individuals, such as New Commonwealth and other economic immigrants, minority ethnic cultural groups, refugees and asylum seekers, Gypsies and Travellers, etc., which have gone unrecognised and have not yet been met by mainstream public services.

- expresses more immediately and directly aspects of individual communities' mutual support, services needs, and political campaigning.

- reflects the cultural, economic and political differences between ethnic communities, as well as mass popular collective campaigning against discrimination and racism.

- provides mutual support and services to minority ethnic communities and new arrivals and refugees.

- promotes race equality and good race relations at local neighbourhood level.

- pressures the public sector to provide better and more sensitive services to local communities.

- undertakes casework with individuals.

Co-ordinating public, private and voluntary and community sector activities.

Relations between the sectors

In recognition of the need to improve collaboration between the public, private, and voluntary and community sectors, and to share there respective merits and strengths, the government has pursued a tripartite strategy of (i) encouraging partnerships between sectors, (ii) blurring the distinction between them by separating service commissioning from service delivery (which can now be undertaken by private sector agencies, as with Private Finance Initiatives (PFI), or not-for-profit companies), and (iii) encouraging greater 'social enterprise' in the voluntary sector. Of these, the new emphasis on collaboration through partnership initiatives has probably had most effect on how promotion of race equality at local level is now conceived and undertaken.

Service improvement through partnership work

In 2001, what was then the Department for Transport, Local Government and the Regions set out a vision for local government in the explicitly-entitled white paper, *Local Leadership – Quality Public Services*, which stressed that local leadership had to be earned through democratic legitimacy, good governance, effective partnership working, meaningful engagement with local communities, and a noticeable improvement in the quality of local services. The government argued that the contribution of the public, private and voluntary sectors, and of local communities themselves, needed to be marshalled in order to tackle the most challenging social problems of health, crime, education, transport, housing and the environment.

Local Strategic Partnerships (LSPs)

One solution was to established Local Strategic Partnerships (LSPs) to develop integrated approaches to local service delivery and to deal with policy priorities in a joined-up way. LSPs, funded through the Neighbourhood Renewal Fund, were set up in the 88 most deprived areas of the country. An LSP is a cross-sectoral, cross-cutting, umbrella partnership aimed at improving the quality of life and governance in a particular locality. It brings together the public, private, and voluntary and community sectors to provide an overarching coordination framework within which other more specific local partnerships can operate. It is intended to improve local public services by bringing those who deliver or commission different services together with those for whom services are provided. The aspiration behind LSPs is to enable all local service providers to 'work with each other, the private sector, and the broader local community to agree a holistic approach to solving problems with a common vision, agreed objectives, pooled expertise and agreed priorities for the allocation of resources' (Community Strategy Team, October, 2000, p.3).

Inclusivity

Every LSP is expected to include public sector representatives, including elected councilors, private sector representatives, voluntary sector representatives and community representatives. Efforts are made to encourage the participation of women, disabled and older people, faith and youth groups, and people from black and minority ethnic communities (ibid, p.16). This can be done by building on existing community networks, such as those of the local race equality councils, which frequently have representation on the LSP or its subgroups.

Promoting race equality through LSPs

LSPs have the potential to combine three mutually-supportive local policy strands. They can improve inclusivity by bringing together public, private, voluntary and community sectors, and ensuring the involvement of people from minority ethnic communities. They can assist in promoting in a strategic manner race equality in service provision as envisaged by the Race Relations (Amendment) Act 2000. They can play a part in developing community and neighborhood renewal strategies to ensure community cohesion. In summary, race equality councils and minority ethnic group representatives on LSPs might play an active and important role in encouraging minority ethnic community groups' engagement in local decision-making, promoting race equality on the LSP agenda by disseminating good practice and providing training, and attempting to align and coordinate the various race equality schemes and policies of public sector partners.

The scope of local race equality work

The Local Strategic Partnership's relationship with the public, private, and voluntary and community sectors

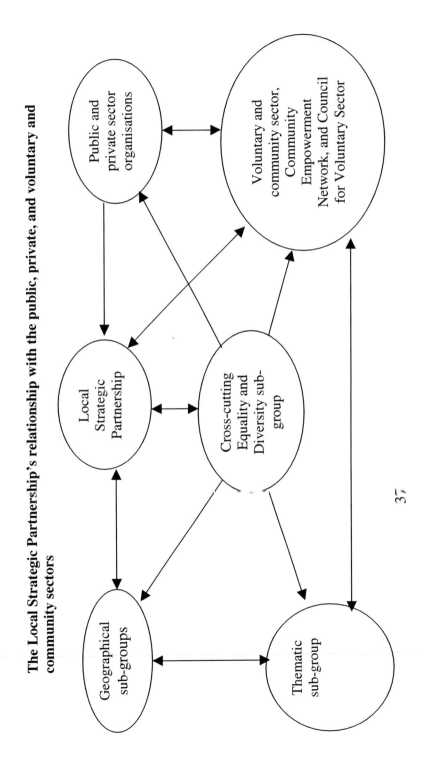

Race equality in local communities

The Local Strategic Partnership and its thematic subgroups

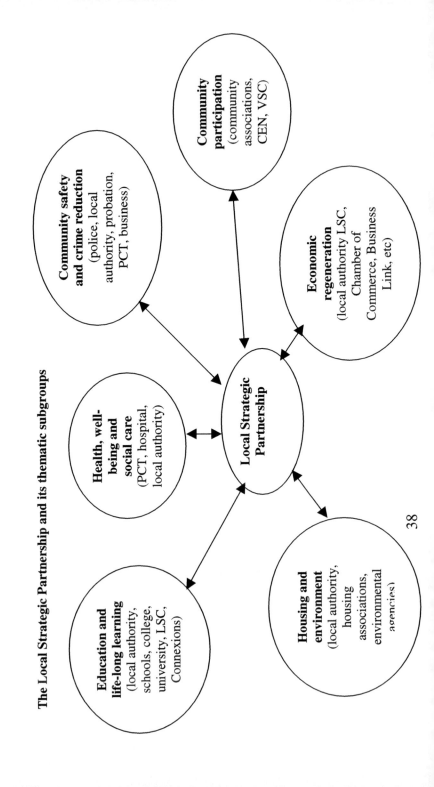

The meaning of 'local'

Throughout this chapter, it is assumed that readers will understand what is meant by 'local', as in the expressions 'local race equality work' and 'local service provision'. Work at local level is being contrasted throughout with work at international, national, or regional level, but 'local' also derives its meaning in this context from its association with the functions and services provided by local government.

In fact, local race equality work is much preoccupied - some would say overly pre-occupied - with policies aimed at improving locally-derived public authority services. When considering the scope of local race equality work, then, it is essential to acquire some understanding of the complexities of British country-wide, regional and local government and where responsibility lies for the various local services on offer. The note that follows provides a beginner's guide. But 'local' is very much a relative concept. A county council, or a large city council, such as Birmingham, may be considered far from local in comparison with a district or neighbourhood. And a district council may be seen as remote and impersonal by people at parish council level, or who relate only to their 'local community'.

Area of benefit

To be effective, local race equality work must negotiate or bridge all these levels. In reality, however, most race equality organisations relate to a constitutionally-limited area of benefit, usually defined in term of local government boundaries, and are supported to some degree by the local authority or authorities operating on that patch. Thus, a race equality organisation is traditionally identified by the name of the unitary authority, county, or district council, for which it provides a benefit. In a two-tier authority, it may be given grants by both county council and district councils. It can, of course, seek funding from other public authorities operating in its area of benefit, or from organisations at regional or national level (such as the CRE), which are legally sanctioned to give grants to local voluntary organisations. At the time of writing, Race Equality West Midlands is the only race equality organisation with a regional brief, but receives no funding from regional agencies.

Country-wide, regional and local government structures

Britain consists of three countries, England, with a population of approximately 50 million people, Scotland with just over 5 million people, and Wales with just under 3 million people. Scotland has a Scottish Parliament whose responsibilities include health, education, and training, local government, housing, economic development, some home affairs, civil and criminal law, transport, environment, agriculture, fisheries, forestry, sports and the arts. The National Assembly for Wales has responsibility for economic development, agriculture, forestry, fisheries, and food, education and training, industry, local government, health and personal social services, housing, environment, planning, transport, roads, arts and culture. England is divided into nine regions each served by a Regional Development Agency (RDA) and a Government Office (GO). One of the English regions, London, has the Greater London Authority which sets key strategies on issues affecting London, such as transport, economic development, strategic and spatial development and the environment. Scotland, Wales and the nine English regions are made up of areas administered by local authorities which have local powers and functions granted to them under various parliamentary acts. There is considerable variation across Britain but, as a rough guide, local authorities are either two tiered or single tiered.

Two-tiered and single-tiered local government

Two-tier systems consist of counties sub-divided into districts. These counties, as well as their constituent districts, have locally-elected councils. County councils provide large-scale services, such as transport, planning, highways, traffic regulation, education, social services, while (county) district councils are responsible for local services such as environmental health, social housing, local planning applications, and collection of refuse. By contrast, unitary authorities, often situated in the major conurbations, and variously referred to as cities, boroughs, or districts (although these labels are not indicators of unitary status) are responsible for all local authority services on their patch (apart from those which are organised across neighbouring areas, such as the fire services and public transport). Partly because of the confusion caused by two-tier divisions of responsibility, there has been a move towards single-tier or unitary authorities, with 46 new unitary authorities established in England in the 1990s.

Other local service providers

While local authorities with locally-elected councils offer a range of local services, it should not be assumed that they run them all, or even those services people consider to be essential. Primary health care is the responsibility of the local Primary Care Trust, hospital treatment that of Hospital trusts. The police service and criminal justice agencies are separate. Housing Associations and so called Arms Length Management organisations (ALMOs) manage social housing tenancies. Local primary and secondary schools have been granted a degree of autonomy from their local education authorities. Other services, such as water, gas, and electricity, usually referred to as utilities, are provided by private companies.

Chapter Two

Local race equality organisations and their functions

Overview. Race equality organisations share the objective of promoting race equality. Six categories of organisation can be distinguished, including those of the race equality councils and the race equality partnerships. Traditional race equality councils have four constitutionally-defined functions: policy development, community support, assistance to individuals and public education. These are functions they are permitted to exercise. Not all have the resources to undertake them in equal measure. Specialisation has resulted in the emergence of different organisational types. Race equality partnerships have been developed as an alternative to race equality councils, and are intended to contribute to service improvement by providing a bridge between service providers and users. Chapter Two also explores the governance and funding arrangements of race equality councils and partnerships.

Kinds of local race equality organisation

Local variation in race equality organisation (REO)

Local race equality organisations (REOs) vary in the functions they perform, the way they are governed and managed, the size of their budgets, the number of staff they have in post, the outcomes they achieve, and their reputation for effectiveness. What they have in common, however, are the primary objectives, (usually enshrined in their constitution) of achieving

43

race equality by working to (i) eliminate racial discrimination and (ii) promote equality of opportunity and good relations between persons of different racial groups. They share these objectives (set out in the Race Relations Act, 1976) with the Commission for Racial Equality. The Crime and Disorder Act 1998 has since encouraged REOs to extend their work on eliminating discrimination to the provision of support for victims of criminal assault and damage.

Six categories of race equality organisations (REOs)

Nowadays, organisations specialising in race equality work take different forms, but usually fit one of the following six categories.

- *Race equality councils (RECs).* They have a broad membership of local community organisations and generally follow the CRE's revised model constitution for race equality councils, 1995.

- *Race equality partnerships (REPs).* Usually, they are formed as a local partnership between voluntary and community organisations, and public authorities (and, less commonly, private sector agencies) and are governed by a small board of trustees and/or directors.

- *Equality partnerships (EPs).* Since proposals were first made to set up the Commission for Equality and Human Rights and to close the Commission for Racial Equality and other

44

commissions at national level, equality partnerships have been mooted, promoted, and in some cases, locally established, despite the ongoing need to resolve the problems of combining the six legally-recognised strands of equality work into a systematic and effective practice.

- *Racial harassment and discrimination advice, guidance, and support agencies and networks (RHNs),*often with a monitoring brief. They are usually run by a committee of local community groups and of members of agencies that have to deal with the negative consequences of harassment and violence.

- *Stand-alone race equality projects.* Sometimes supported by public authorities, they have been set up to deal with a specific local task, for example, advising complainants of discrimination, engaging in specific ethnic minority health, education or community-safety projects.

- *Second-tier umbrella organisations.* Operating at a national or regional level, examples are the British Federation of Race Equality Councils and Race Equality West Midlands.

Partnerships replacing councils

Race equality councils remain the commonest form of local race equality organisation in Britain, but most, if not all, newly-established bodies have been set up as partnerships. Many recent partnerships have also been 'future proofed' to take on broader equality remits, not only for race. For some time, too, especially since the CRE began to disengage from the funding of REC posts and the supervision of work programmes, the need for a collective race equality infrastructure has been recognised, such as that provided by Race Equality West Midlands, although regional funding for it has not until recently been available. This gap has been filled in part by private consultants brought in by REOs and local authorities to undertake specific development tasks.

Difference between race equality organisations and black and minority ethnic pressure groups.

Race equality organisations operate in a crowded context of competing voluntary and community agencies offering a wide range of community services irrespective of race or colour or, as in the case of minority ethnic community groups, self-help and mutual support for persons of a specific ethnicity. While frequently understood as contributing to racial equality in addressing service deficits for disadvantaged ethnic minorities, they are not organisations with a primary purpose of promoting race equality for all ethnic groups (majority and minority) living in local geographically-defined communities. REOs have found it difficult to explain (i) that race equality promotion is something more than promoting minority ethnic interests and (ii) that racial inequality has unique distinguishing features that cannot be dealt with simply by adopting an undifferentiated generic approach to bringing about greater equality.

Local race equality organisations and their functions

Race Equality Councils (RECs)

The four constitutionally-explicit functions of RECs

According to the CRE's model REC constitution (1995), race equality councils aim to fulfil their purpose by engaging in policy development, community support, assistance to individuals and public education.

Policy development

Policy development is explained as acquainting organisations, in the statutory, non-statutory, private, and voluntary sectors with the extent and nature of racial discrimination and inequality experienced by racial groups in the field of social welfare, and in particular, the fields of housing, employment, education and health care, with the aim of encouraging them to implement policies and practices which will eliminate racial discrimination and promote equality of opportunity and good relations between persons of different racial groups. (Chapter Five deals in greater detail with race equality policy development.)

Community support

Community support involves helping organisations which are concerned with the promotion of equal opportunity and good relations between persons of different racial groups, by providing them with information, advice and other forms of assistance in keeping with REC objectives.   (Chapter Seven

47

focuses on supporting communities and improving race relations.)

Assistance to individuals

RECs are expected to give information, advice, and support (including representation at tribunals) of a non-financial nature to individuals who seek the REC's assistance as a consequence of their experience of racism or racial discrimination (where that information and advice and support are not readily available from other local agencies).(Chapter Nine describes REC case work.)

Public education

RECs are expected to maintain an appropriate programme of public information and education related to the REC's aims and functions. (Chapter Ten deals with how to go about explaining race relations.)

Permissible versus actual reported REC functions

The four constitutionally-sanctioned REC functions described above are interpreted, developed and implemented by RECs in different ways. There is a difference between what RECs are constitutionally permitted to do in relation to their general aims and what they do in practice. A REWM survey in 2001 showed that RECs differed widely in the work they prioritised and involved themselves in.

Race Equality Councils: reported functions

Functions	% of RECs
Policy development	
Equal opportunity policy development for public, private and voluntary sector	90
Community policy development in partnership with public authorities and other agencies	72
Consultation exercises undertaken for public authorities	72
Monitoring of local organisations' equal opportunity policy	63
Community support	
Involvement in community development/capacity building projects	78
Participation in regeneration initiatives	63
Race relations and community needs/local needs analyses	50
Local 'watchdog', exposing cases of racial injustice and disadvantage	63
Law enforcement, anti-crime, criminal justice, victim support initiatives	63
Assistance to individuals	
Information and advice to individuals	78
Casework with complaints	63
Tribunal representation of complaints	22
Support for victims of racial harassment and violence	72
Public education	
Campaigns to raise public awareness of racism and race related issues	59
Cultural, community, educational and	59

life-long learning projects	
Responses to local media exposure/events inimical to good race relations	50

Source: REWM: returns from 32 of 88 RECs, July 2001.

REC functions listed in more detail

In the 2004 national audit of RECs and REPs (RED 9, REWM 2004, p. 11), the following twenty-six, sometimes overlapping, functions and services were listed by respondents in answer to the question as to what they had to offer:

advice and information
advocacy
assisting black and minority ethnic groups
asylum seeker\refugee support
brokerage
careers advice
casework
community capacity-building
community cohesion work
community development
community engagement
community partnerships
complainant aid
conflict mediation
criminal justice policy development
education advice (including work with schools and colleges)
employment discrimination casework
immigration advice

projects on race equality
public awareness-raising and education
public policy work
reporting racial incidents
support for victims of racial harassment
training on equality and diversity
translation and interpreting
youth work.

Newly-specified REC functions under old headings

The range of services offered by RECs has expanded since the model constitution was written but recent additions can still be presented under the old headings:

Policy development

- Assisting public authorities with their duties to promote race equality under the Race Relations (Amendment) Act, 2000.

Community support

- Establishing partnerships with the public, private and voluntary and community sectors to improve the quality and sensitivity of service delivery.

- Managing and undertaking local community development or regeneration projects, usually involving black and minority ethnic communities, but now increasingly aimed at building bridges between groups divided along ethnic lines (often referred to as 'building community cohesion').

- Mediating between the parties to inter-ethnic community conflict.

Assistance to individuals

- Assisting people who believe they have suffered from racial discrimination in taking complaints to employment tribunals and the civil courts under the Race Relations Act.

- Helping victims of racial harassment and violence.

Public education

- Raising public awareness of racial and ethnic issues and the benefits of cultural diversity, often in the context of concurrent racist political campaigning.

- Contributing to citizenship education.

Most frequently-mentioned REC functions and services

The most frequently-mentioned services were (i) assisting public authorities (with their race equality schemes), (ii) public policy work (often relating to the Race Relations (Amendment) Act 2000), (iii) training on equality and diversity, (iv) support for victims of racial harassment and discrimination, (v) public awareness-raising and education, (vi) casework and complainant aid, and (vii) community development (in descending order of frequency of mention) (ibid, p.11).

KPMG review of RECs, 1997

In 1997, the consultancy firm, KPMG, was asked by the CRE to undertake a review of the public-service functions of racial equality councils. On the whole, the review portrayed RECs in an extremely positive light, confirming their important contribution to local racial equality work. KPMG's conclusions were cautiously framed, but appeared to raise more questions about the CRE's failure to provide strategic leadership to the RECs, than about their effectiveness (CRE 1997).

Lack of CRE strategy and support for RECs

KPMG did not think that the CRE had set out a clear strategy on complainant aid services with which it cooperated with local RECs in providing. There seemed to be no rationale for CRE investment in alternative complainant aid projects, no guidance on how RECs should work with other aid projects, no investments in supporting RECs to undertake the specialised nature of the work through reference manuals, case updates, shadowing, etc. absence of any guidance on how lessons from casework might be used to develop a wider race equality strategy, a variable relationship between the RECs and the CRE in terms of cross-referrals, etc., and little by way of national or regional training schemes in tribunal representation.

Importance of RECs' local contribution

KPMG believed that RECs were a vital point of access for many individual complainants and that the CRE should target investment at designated REC centres of complainant-aid expertise. KPMG also saw RECs as playing an important role in local public education and policy development work, recommending that the CRE's national and regional planning should recognise the nature of RECs' local contribution. The CRE, it felt, should accept that many priorities were best determined locally. The review concluded that there was a clear need for a distinctly local racial equality service which, by demonstrating its grounding in local communities, was able to secure recognition from other key local agencies.

The need for local race equality strategy and flexible arrangements

By coming down so firmly in favour of locally-based racial equality work, KPMG also drew attention to the need for RECs to plan their work strategically, renewing their objects and modes of operation in the context of local requirements, the setting of specific targets, and the mobilisation of the resources necessary to achieve them. RECs should be allowed to experiment, if they wished, with formal changes to electoral or constitutional arrangements in order to secure a greater level of representation in their membership. The CRE acted on some of KPMG's recommendations, for example, by attempting to rationalise the provision of complainant aid and encouraging the development of REPs.

Other inexplicit REC functions

Apart from the explicit functions, it is quite apparent from actual reported functions and the changing nature of REC work, that RECs have always had, or have acquired in response to the changing external environment, a number of other attributes that are not reflected in their formal constitutions. Variously selected and categorised, the most obvious are their roles in mediating, resolving and controlling racial, ethnic and related conflict, in coordinating the drive for race equality and developing strategy in respect of its promotion, in establishing minority ethnic community service needs through research, and in marketing services.

Mediating, resolving and controlling racial, ethnic and other conflict.

RECs have always been expected to contribute to diffusing racial tension. They have periodically been castigated when, instead, they have taken the side of angry ethnic communities in opposition to the authorities, especially the police (see the Scarman report 1981). In situations of racial and ethnic conflict, RECs have in the main been prevailed upon to play a de-escalatory mediating role, pleading for order in the face of confrontation by community activists. Community expectations may have been disappointed and REC reputation lost as a consequence of their abject peace-making efforts, but they have usually managed to stay in business. Their role in contributing to conflict management has once more been brought to the fore by the 2001 disturbances in northern England and their aftermath.

Coordinative and strategic role

Chapter One situated the race equality promotional activities of RECs at the heart of local strategic networks. It is increasingly recognised that in order to make any significant and enduring impact on racial inequality, it is essential to agree common goals and to engage in collaborative action with other like-minded agencies and community organisations. In regard to race equality promotional strategy, RECs were until recently content to accept the leadership of the CRE (which funded them) and to adopt its priorities when planning their work programmes. The broad strategy had essentially been set at national level following the Policy Studies Institute's review of the role and objectives of Community Relations Councils (1988) and in the implementation of the CRE response to it (1989). The KMPG report (CRE 1997) criticised the CRE for not providing that strategic leadership and suggested that RECs should review their objectives in the context of local conditions and develop their own strategies. In the West Midlands, the strategic Race Equality Forum of RECs and REPs was established to undertake this task and its members work within a strategic and infrastructural development framework.

Establishing minority ethnic needs through research.

An essential feature of modern management is its commitment to evidence-based decision-making.

Increasingly, RECs are expected to keep comprehensive records of all their transactions and to monitor and assess their performance using the feedback to modify and improve their practice. It is taken for granted that managers in today's RECs should operate in this cyclical manner if they are to deliver and improve race equality services. The output model of performance implies that race equality work should, where possible, be based on prior research findings, and the result evaluated to see whether intervention was indeed effective. RECs have for many years made use of race relations research, of course, but have increasingly become involved in collecting their own data as evidence to support their work, and assigning time and resources to compilation, circulation, and dissemination.

The marketing function

It has been believed for some time that the techniques of marketing could usefully be extended from the commercial sector to public services and not-for-profit organisations. (Kinnell and MacDougall, 1977). This would, it is thought, enable organisations, such as REOs, to meet the needs of client groups more effectively and to achieve desirable social change (such as improving standards of health and education). Organisations with a market orientation focus on analysing and satisfying their customers' or users' needs. According to this approach, an REO should not start out with a prior work programme or project, but consult with local communities to discover what it ought to be doing. Individuals have wants (specific desires directed towards fulfilling their basic needs) and marketing approaches aim to satisfy these wants. In an organisation based on a philosophy of marketing, staff are primarily focused on assessing customer (user) wants, gathering marketing intelligence, ensuring they have access to and take up the service made available, and obtaining and assessing their reaction to or satisfaction with it.

REO marketing strategy

REOs can probably learn a great deal from the ideas of marketing and go on to develop a marketing strategy. This involves specifying as clearly as possible their main 'customers' (e.g. complainants of discrimination, public authorities, minority ethnic community organisations and groups, religious and faith groups), and service range (case work, consultancy, training, research). REOs would also need to decide who their competitors were and what channels of communication and distribution they could best make use of. Consciousness of marketing principles could result in greatly improved services and increased user satisfaction. The marketing approach relates closely to the idea of REOs as media hubs (see Chapter Ten).

Specialised types or styles of REC

RECs have always adapted their work in response to local conditions and the resources available to them. They have frequently been forced to specialise in one or more areas of service provision and now rarely undertake the full range of activities (at the same level of intensity) as permitted by the model constitution. Four main service types or styles are distinguishable.

Local race equality organisations and their functions

Type 1: Consultancy and training service for public authorities or voluntary agencies on race equality and equality of opportunity policy. (Alternatively, a pressure group for improving services to black and minority ethnic communities.)

Type 2: Community development agency seeking to empower and/or build the capacity of local black and minority ethnic groups or communities, or more recently, to improve relations and build bridges between all the different ethnic communities living in an area.

Type 3: Professional support bureau for complainants of unlawful discrimination, discrimination generally, or the victims of racial harassment and violence.

Type 4: Public awareness and education service (often delivered in partnership with local schools, colleges, libraries, or youth service). (In practice, this type is not found separately but in combination with any of the other three.)

Recent REC development and specialisation

Far fewer RECs now specialise in complainant aid (Type 3), as it is resource-intensive and, in recent years, has not been a CRE funding priority. Many RECs have found it easier to acquire community development grants and have increasingly focused their work on delivering community development and cohesion projects (Type 2). This may explain why they were seen in the White Paper on the Commission for Equality and Human Rights as playing a major role in community bridge-building, ironically, the main and much-criticised purpose of their predecessors, the Community Relations Councils. In the context of the duty placed on public authorities to promote race equality, many RECs have also aspired to playing a greater role in assisting public authorities (Type 1), but have not always had the capacity, nor been strategically well-placed, to do so.

RECs as service providers

Along with others in the voluntary and community sector, RECs are publicly viewed as organisations whose primary purpose is to provide a service, in their case, a race equality service, free and on the basis of need, rather than on individuals' ability to pay. RECs have been forced to emphasise their role as service providers, partly to secure funding and charitable status, and partly because another historically-significant function that they perform has been taken for granted or ignored.

RECs as community forums

RECs were never originally conceived as direct providers of services, but as community-expressive forums to enable spokespersons for newly-arrived minority ethnic groups, and those progressive elements in the population who were concerned to ensure such groups were fairly treated, to articulate, aggregate and advance the collective community interest. The aim was to improve the treatment of ethnic minorities by informing and educating the general public and bringing political pressure to bear on firms and public service providers which discriminated or contributed to the disadvantage of minority ethnic individuals.

The meaning of 'council'

The original Councils for Racial Harmony and Community Relations Councils were conceived as 'councils', in the sense that they deliberated about, and spoke out in support of, improving ethnic and race relations, and formed a kind of alternative local parliament on behalf of what were then the most politically-marginalised sections of the population. In the context of the Race Relations Act 1976 and the growing reliance on government and local authority funding sources, RECs have increasingly asserted their functions as service providers, while downplaying their community-expressive political role.

REC functions reflected in organisational shape

The organisational shape of RECs, however, continues to reflect their historical community-expressive dimension. There is a diverse membership of organisations including local black and minority ethnic organisations. A large executive committee provides governance for much smaller numbers of paid staff. REC staff spend a great deal of their time arranging and servicing council executive and sub-committee meetings, as well as managing service delivery. There is a sense in which the government has begun to acknowledge the earlier community-expressive agenda of the RECs with its new emphasis on the importance of Community Empowerment Networks (CENs). The community-expressive dimension of race equality work plays little part in current assessment of RECs' contribution to local race relations and communities. RECs are now judged on the services they provide, not on the contribution they make as participatory bodies.

Race Equality Partnerships (REPs)

REP development in a context of service improvement initiatives

Race equality partnerships (REPs) have usually been inaugurated to help public authorities improve their services to black and minority ethnic communities through joined-up working, and to contribute to the effectiveness of community development, regeneration and empowerment initiatives. A REP is intended to form a bridge between service providers and users, assisting and strengthening government initiatives to improve service standards and quality of life in a particular administrative area or neighbourhood.

Engaging voluntary and community groups in decision-making

A REP is often seen as a means of engaging a wider range of voluntary and community groups (especially 'excluded' or 'hard-to-reach' populations) in local decision-making and regeneration. There has been a tendency, however, to focus on the issues of public service improvement and the eradication of institutional racism from the point of view of the more powerful public agencies participating in the partnership, sometimes at the expense of grass-roots community development, casework with individuals, or victim support.

REPs replacing RECs

REPs vary a great deal in purpose and functions, partner membership, operation and outcome. Many have replaced race equality councils either as a result of a deliberate REC strategy of renewal or because the REC failed. Of thirteen race equality organisations in the West Midlands region, for example, eight now have constitutions based on a partnership approach.

Streamlining governance or undermining community accountability?

REPs are sometimes seen as having the advantage of streamlined and strengthened governance, avoiding the often ponderous business of mediating between entrenched or incompatible local community interests. Community organisations, however, may view REPs with suspicion, seeing them as a means of reducing community control. The partnership approach is currently being explored as a possible answer to how multi-strand equality work might be undertaken at local level.

Influence of other partnerships

REP development has often been informed by and modelled on the formation of other partnerships at local level, particularly, in recent years, Local Strategic Partnerships and their thematic sub-groups. These are intended to bring the major public providers together to coordinate their services and to make them more responsive to community need.

The theory of insider status

In theory, by creating a unitary purpose between the partners, reflected at director, management and operational levels, the REP can gain unrivalled insider entry into and influence over race policy in public and private organisations, in contrast to the community-dominated REC with its outsider status and reputation for criticism from the sidelines. The counter-argument is that the REP is more likely to be induced into adopting a less-than-critical stance towards its more powerful members' faults. Anecdotal evidence suggests powerful institutional partners wield considerable influence on REP boards and are likely to veto action they do not approve of, particularly action critical of them.

Statement of REP objectives and functions

The main and most commonly occurring objectives and functions of REPs can be formally stated as follows:

Policy development

- To facilitate collaboration between the public, private and community sectors, by means of the Local Strategic Partnerships and other thematic, geographical and cross-cutting partnerships, in order to promote race equality, encourage inclusivity and improve community cohesiveness.

- To assist local service providers to work individually, and in partnership with one another, the private sector, and the broader community, to ensure their services are delivered in an holistic manner, free of institutional racism and discrimination.

- To advise and assist public authorities on their general and specific duties under the Race Relations (Amendment) Act 2000 and, where appropriate, to monitor and scrutinise their performance in relation to the legislation.

- To assist in identifying, assessing, and monitoring functions and policies that impact on race equality, consulting groups that may be affected by those functions and policies, and making available information about the outcomes of assessment, consultation and monitoring exercises, and the benefits or services available.

Community development

- To engage with, and participate actively in plans, programmes and services aimed at alleviating disadvantage and discrimination and improving social conditions.

- To play an active role in local forums and community networks aimed at involving members of local communities in the decision-making processes that affect their lives.

- To encourage, support and empower groups, such as women, disabled and other persons, faith and youth groups, and people from black and minority ethnic communities.

- To contribute to community cohesion by playing an active part in developing a common vision, a sense of belonging, an appreciation of diversity, and strong and positive relationships between people from different backgrounds in local schools, colleges, places of work and residential neighbourhoods.

Casework

- Either separately, as a free-standing service, or in partnership with (an) other agency(ies), to give information, advice and other support to individuals who seek assistance as a consequence of their experience of unlawful discrimination, particularly of a racial kind, in circumstances where such information, advice and support are not readily obtainable from other local agencies.

- To offer help and support to victims of racial harassment, intimidation, and violence, and other racially-motivated crime.

- To monitor closely incidents of discrimination and racially motivated crime, with a view to providing information and advice to public authorities on measures that might be taken to reduce their number.

Public information and education

- To provide information and education to members of the public and to local organisations, especially those who are members of the Local Strategic Partnership, on race and community relations, with a view to dispelling misconceptions and stereotypes and promoting understanding and tolerance.

- To monitor national, regional and local media news, views and opinion about racial groups and their relations and to take action to redress misinformation and promote positive reporting about the benefits of living in a multi-racial environment.

- To monitor and take effective action against the propaganda, behaviour and campaigning of extreme nationalist and racist groups that oppose the Race Relations Act and other anti-discrimination legislation and seek to undermine good race relations and the cohesion of local communities.

General

- To undertake any other similar function compatible with the general objects.

- To work closely and in collaborative partnership with other race equality organisations within the region to fulfil these functions.

(These functions are derived from the draft constitution prepared by REWM for Race Equality Sandwell. We wish to thank Race Equality Sandwell for its permission to reproduce this list.)

Race equality organisation governance and structure

RECs as membership organisations

RECs are membership organisations. Their membership is open to any incorporated association (affiliate membership) and individuals (individual membership) which/who are interested in furthering its work. Affiliate members must make a written declaration of their commitment and satisfy the REC that there is nothing in their constitution which conflicts with the REC's aims. Individual members must also make a formal declaration of their commitment. RECs, therefore, have an open membership, providing those who seek to join agree with their aims.

REC executive committee

The REC membership of associations and individuals elects an executive committee, consisting of between 18 and 25 members of whom two thirds must be elected by ballot of members at the annual general meeting. Honorary officers (chair, vice-chair, secretary and treasurer) are chosen by the executive committee.

Sub-committees

The executive committee must appoint a finance and general purposes sub-committee and personnel sub-committee. A membership panel will receive, consider and determine membership applications, as well as recommend to the executive committee any termination of membership. The executive committee can set up other sub-committees, ad hoc working parties, and task groups. The executive committee decides on the REC's strategic direction, deals with its financial and legal affairs, and is able to employ full-time staff.

Charity and company registration

Many RECs have registered as charities and/or companies to gain financial and legal benefits, such as exemption from tax or business rates, a limitation on the liability of members, and a greater eligibility to access government or charitable funds.

REP partnership boards

REPs are usually governed by a board of directors and/or trustees. Board membership is nearly always smaller than that of a REC executive committee. Board members are frequently nominated by constituencies that are treated as being representative of the public, private, voluntary and community sectors. Board members from public authorities, for example, might be nominated by each of the major public authorities operating in the area or, alternatively, by public sector representatives participating in the Local Strategic Partnership. Private sector nominations might be made by the Chamber of Commerce. The voluntary and community representatives might come by way of Councils for Voluntary Service, Black and Minority Ethnic Forums, Community Empowerment Networks, or specially-established stakeholder groups.

REPs not membership organisations

Some boards might seek nominations on a periodic or rolling basis, while others might renew their composition only when vacancies occur because of resignation or failure of attendance. The crucial difference between most REPs and RECs, is that the former are not membership organisations and do not automatically hold elections among their members to fill their official positions. Such elections that do take place will be for honorary officer posts at board level.

Example of REP governance arrangements

As governance arrangements vary, it is instructive to look at two examples, the first with a more tightly-controlled board membership, the second with membership determined by constituencies. The first has a board of ten directors, consisting of five agencies (City Council, Trades Council, Voluntary Services Council, Learning and Skills Council, and Primary Care Trust) and five community representatives selected in its area of benefit. The second has a board of seventeen, consisting of an appointed independent chair, and four directors each from four constituencies: representatives of the public sector nominated by the LSP, representatives of the voluntary sector nominated by the CVS, representatives of local communities nominated by a 'community stake-holder' group and representatives from the private sector and wider regional interests, nominated by the Chamber of Commerce and wider regional interests.

REPs as companies and charities

Unlike some of the earlier established RECs, these new organisations are invariably set up as both companies limited by guarantee and registered charities, and they operate to standard memoranda and articles of association, which also act as their constitution. They have the normal company powers to appoint staff and manage their financial affairs within the scope of the law.

The funding of race equality organisations (REOs)

Traditional funding arrangements

Local race equality councils and their predecessors, community relations councils, were originally funded in roughly equal proportions by their local authority and the Commission for Racial Equality (an arrangement initiated by its predecessor, the Commission for Community Relations). The local authority often provided accommodation and administrative support, with the Commission funding race equality officer posts. Long after the CRE ceased funding posts in favour of simply making block grants to RECs in support of local officer salaries, fossil traces of the old arrangements could be detected in the proportion of the grant still allocated towards race equality officer pension costs. The CRE/REC pension scheme was finally closed in 2005.

Section 44 of the Race Relations Act 1976

Local authorities and the CRE continue, however, to provide funding to local REOs. Section 44 of the Race Relations Act 1976 allows the CRE, with the approval of the Secretary of State, to give financial and other assistance to any organisation concerned with the promotion of equality of opportunity, and good relations between persons of different racial groups. The money is now used to purchase services conceived as outcomes, and no longer supports particular posts.

CRE Getting Results grant aid

From 2002-03 onwards, the CRE introduced a system of grant aid referred to as *Getting Results.* It is awarded on the basis of applications from race equality and other organisations to deliver annually-agreed outcomes, milestones and outputs against CRE priorities. For 2007-08, organisations could apply for up to three outcomes at £33,500 per outcome per annum.

Other funding sources

Given the short-term nature of grant aid and the uncertainty surrounding funding, established local race equality organisations have been under pressure to find new ways of resourcing their activities.

Local race equality organisations and their functions

REWM's 2004 national audit of REOs showed that local organisations had often succeeded in diversifying their funding base, with income coming from seven sources: the CRE (20%), local councils (40%), other public authorities (10%), National Lottery (10%), regeneration funds (5%), own income generation (5%), and other (10%).

Variation between race equality organisations in income and income sources

There was, however, a great deal of variation between REOs, the more successful having a larger number of income streams and being less dependent on the traditional sources of local authority and CRE. In one region, the proportion of CRE funding had fallen to 10%, with national lottery grants accounting for a third, and government regeneration initiatives for a quarter, of all REO income.

Annual variations in income

Most REOs report problems in managing annual variations in their income, which result in uncertainty, staff turnover, and difficulties in sustaining regular work programmes. Increasingly, REOs find themselves delivering a plethora of outputs, outcomes and targets to sustain their income, with little flexibility for manoeuvre within the confines of previously-agreed project outcomes and restricted funding.

Concept of core costs

A recurring observation is that there is insufficient funding available to cover the core costs of keeping the organisation going. Core costs could, or should, be provided for in the costing of outcomes, but seldom are, as most public funding is severely limited and REOs have little choice but to accept what is on offer, even if delivery results in a deficit. Outcome-related funding is invariably time-limited, with no guarantee of repetition or renewal, thus contributing further to the financial uncertainty and instability currently endemic in the voluntary sector.

The search for sustainable and regular income

Time has increasingly to be spent on the search for funding, variously estimated at between a fifth and a third of managers' time. Nearly all successful REOs have grown as a result of the exercise of entrepreneurial and related political skills by their chief executives. But success brings its own problems. The sustainability of the income thus generated is also a matter of concern. Rapid expansion, followed by equally-rapid contraction, is a particularly destructive scenario, leading to de-motivation and low morale.

The future: funding contingent on service contracts?

REO managers and their boards find themselves torn between the traditional ethos of charitable public service responding to need and the recognition that they must operate as a surplus-generating business venture, taking on only economically-viable projects and causes. In the context of public authorities increasingly refashioning themselves as purchasers (or commissioners) of services from providers in any of the three sectors, race equality organisations may have to adjust to the prospect of competing in the guise of new-style social enterprises for service contracts. Currently, of course, public authority procurement policy generally favours larger providers, standardised corporate contracts, and economies of scale. But are race equality organisations simply providers of services, or, in Handy's terms, shouldn't they endeavour to retain their self-help and campaigning roles?

Social enterprises

In November 2006, the government launched proposals to encourage the development of social enterprises in the social space believed to exist between traditional charitable foundations motivated by philanthropic intent and private businesses driven by the need to make profit for shareholders. Social enterprises may provide public authorities with the solution to improving services while simultaneously achieving value for money. The concept derives from the cooperative and mutual societies which used a business model for collective self-help. It is too soon to decide whether the organisational model emerging is relevant to the development of REOs.

Chapter Three

Working for a local race equality organisation

Overview. Race equality organisations (REOs) operate to annual work programmes often based on three-year strategic or business plans, setting out the outcomes they are expected to deliver. Five categories of person come together to deliver these outcomes: members, staff, consultants, volunteers, and trainees, all of whom have a unique contribution to make to race equality work. Within the organisation, there is a division of labour and a degree of specialisation reflected in the staffing structures, job titles and job descriptions. Five basic principles operate in deciding how tasks, roles and responsibilities are shared out. Examples are given of typical jobs. Two perspectives are offered on the kinds of knowledge, values and skills that are required to undertake successful race equality work: the intuitive experiential and the rational expert. The latter perspective now dominates, as evidenced by the increasing numbers of race equality staff qualified to degree level in relevant disciplines. The chapter concludes by setting out factors critical to the success of local REOs.

Organisational and personal work programmes

Most REOs operate to an annually-revised organisational work programme systematically setting out the tasks that have to be undertaken and the milestones reached to deliver a set of agreed outcomes, the achievement of which is measured against more tangible, visible or measurable outputs. The general organisational work programme often makes clear personal responsibilities for ensuring particular tasks are undertaken and outcomes achieved, but sometimes personalised work programmes are also devised and issued to individual race equality personnel.

Five categories of person

Members

The outcomes of REOs are normally delivered by several of five categories of person: members (including directors), staff, consultants, volunteers, and trainees. Members, particularly executive committee members and directors, undertake a great deal of unpaid work relating to governance and general decision-making, oversight of financial affairs and signing of cheques, chairing public meetings and panels, consulting and negotiating with various stakeholders, appraising the performance of senior staff and participating in serious disciplinary hearings, representing the public face and interests of the organisation, and advising the chief executive on strategy.

Value of board member input

Members, honorary officers and/or directors are usually required to agree the strategic direction, expenditure, work programme and grant applications of the organisation. It is easy to forget, but the hard work and loyal support of board members are essential to a voluntary sector organisation's success.

Failure, indeed, is often a consequence of a factionalised and warring executive committee or board of directors.

Staff

The staff of the organisation are responsible for the delivery of the greater part of the work programme. Unless agreed outcomes are successfully delivered on time to the specification of stakeholders supporting the organisation, funding for subsequent years will be at risk, and claw-back of existing money a distinct possibility. It is essential, therefore, that the work programme is realistic in its expectations and matched closely to staff numbers, time, skills, experience and ability.

REOs' staffing complements

REOs vary in the number of staff they employ. The REWM 2004 national audit showed that RECs/REPs employed an average of 8.25 staff, with numbers ranging from one to twenty-five. This figure corresponded closely with that obtained from the 2003 West Midlands audit, but disguises the large differences in organisations' staffing complements. One fifth were 'singleton', that is having only one generalist race equality officer, either with or without administrative support. What might reasonably be expected of a singleton will be less than of an organisation of 25, although the size of the staffing complement is often forgotten when performance comes to be assessed.

Working for a local race equality organisation

Fixed-term staff contracts

Staff may be full-time or vary in the number of part-time hours they work, but a significant feature of voluntary-sector race equality employment is the number of staff – nearly three fifths or 57% - on fixed-term or temporary contracts. A majority is working on projects with a short funding life, not usually of more than three years. Apart from being insecure, contracts of this kind have other adverse consequences. Frequently, they do not attract an employer pension contribution and obtaining a mortgage or loan may prove difficult. A small minority of staff – around 5% - has been seconded to RECs/REPs from other agencies, sometimes to circumvent problems of attracting competent staff on poor conditions.

Negative effects of fixed-term and temporary contracts

The effect on staff and race equality work of fixed-term and temporary contractual arrangements is predictable. Managers claim that it is difficult to attract high calibre, professionally-qualified staff and that job insecurity leads to demotivation and a high turnover as contracts reach full-term. Staff often leave before they acquire the essential training and skills, or establish the local contacts and long-term relationships to do the job effectively. Short-termism hinders commitment, teamwork and the emergence of professionalism. More immediately, it is often difficult to complete projects satisfactorily when staff leave early in anticipation of their contracts drawing to an end. The inability to attract, retain and train staff, or to plan a longer-term staff development strategy, not only adversely affects REO competence and achievement, but undermines the perception and reputation of race equality work as a whole.

Benefits of working in an REO

Nevertheless, it would be wrong to view employment in this sector in only a negative light. The work is often varied, worthwhile and interesting, allowing individual race equality workers scope for innovation. By definition, it involves contact with a diverse range of individuals and groups and provides the kind of stimulation and sense of commitment to a worthwhile endeavour that those who are initially attracted to the work almost inevitably find personally fulfilling and addictive.

Staffing structure

REOs with larger complements of staff will have in place a staffing structure distinguishing levels of responsibility and specialist roles, and represented by a line-management diagram. For small organisations, line management is a relatively simple matter, with main grade project staff answering to project leaders accountable in turn to an executive officer (or an assistant eo) who coordinates all the organisation's activities and is directly accountable to the chair and board of directors (or executive committee). Administrators or clerical assistants will be allocated to particular projects or to a member or members of the senior management team.

Staff categories

The structure thus outlined distinguishes the following categories of staff or employee: chief executive officer (ceo), assistant ceo, project managers, project officers, administrator, and clerical assistants. The way they relate in a management hierarchy can be seen as a pyramidal or lozenge-shape formation.

Consultants

Consultants are persons, partnerships or incorporated bodies hired on contract by an organisation to perform a specialist task or role, either as a one-off exercise or to provide a long-term recurrent service. Given the temporary and fluctuating nature of most race equality organisations' income, which is often geared to the delivery of specific projects and outcomes, one way of avoiding extended commitments and fixed costs is to take on consultants to meet sudden increases in the work load. The use of consultants is also a means of acquiring expertise that is in unavailable among the existing staff, where demand or funding is insufficient to warrant the creation of a specialist post. Consultants can also undertake independent diagnoses and evaluations of an organisation's internal arrangements where a professional or external opinion is legally or politically expedient.

Functions of consultants in REOs

Currently, REOs use consultants to undertake a whole range of functions such as auditing, project evaluation, financial management, legal advice and contract preparation, staff recruitment, writing of funding applications, and the delivery of discrete race equality outcomes, often requiring expertise. Private consultants are frequently hired by local authorities to review the provision or delivery of race equality services within their area prior to setting up a (race) equality organisation or withdrawing funding from an existing one.

Volunteers

Volunteers play a vital part in the success of many race equality projects. Projects, such as the Jigsaw mentoring project at East Staffordshire Race Equality Council, may involve the recruitment of large numbers of volunteers, who, in the case of this example, act as mentors to the project beneficiaries. Volunteers, who may also be REO members, often help to form a bridge between the organisation and the local communities it has been set up to serve.

Motivation of volunteers

Volunteering for race equality work can be variously motivated: some students come for work experience, partly because they are indeed interested in promoting race equality, and partly because it enhances their curriculum vitae. Where volunteering is institutionally recognised (with policies, procedures and protocols in place) and built in as part of project delivery, managers speak in glowing terms of its contribution to the success of the organisation.

Paying volunteers

Payment can be made to particular promising student volunteers who demonstrate they are making a positive impact on the organisation. This arrangement helps to support them while they are still studying and is a means of retaining contact and perhaps encouraging them to consider a career in race equality promotion when they complete their course of study.

Trainees

Recognising the important contribution that part-time paid volunteers might make to the organisation, some REOs have offered them systematic staff development and training in race equality promotion, with a view to their eventually taking up appointment in the field. Capable trainees can add value to the organisation at little extra cost, while at the same time acquiring marketable skills to their own benefit in fund-raising, public relations, project management, the promotion of race, diversity and community cohesion, and much else. One trainee in a Midlands REO secured £50,000 of project funding by developing an idea, writing a properly-budgeted application, and steering the initiative through to success.

External and internal variation between REOs

Although REOs all share the general task of promoting race equality, they operate in local external contexts, ranging from urban to rural, and serve authorities varying in political hue and policy preference and in the ethnic composition of communities with different needs. Internally, too, organisations diverge in their blend of board member, manager, and officer knowledge, skill, experience and competency. They have also sought and been awarded grant aid to undertake a wide range of projects and to achieve outcomes in relation to specifically-targeted beneficiary groups. REOs will vary, therefore, in their line-management structure and in the posts and roles they create and allocate to members, staff, consultants, and volunteers.

REO post titles (2004)

The 2004 national audit of REOs provided a varied list of post titles, including:

Directly race equality-related

Capacity builder, career advisor, caseworker, community access worker, community cohesion officer, community development officer or worker, complainant aid worker, Connecting Communities officer, Connexions youth officer, education officer, employment officer/coordinator, health project coordinator, immigration advice officer, immigration advisor, legal aid officer, mentoring project manager, partnership officer, racial harassment officer/coordinator, race equality chief executive, race equality officer, research officer, sport development officer, surgery advisor, volunteer coordinator.

Supportive roles

Administrative assistant, administrative officer, administrator, business manager, cleaner, finance officer, office manager, personal assistant, receptionist, secretary, senior administrator, training administrator.

Division of labour, specialisation

At least five principles can be detected for deciding on a rational basis how REO tasks, roles and responsibilities are to be shared out, but in practice, and for expediency, these are often modified or combined. Posts may be defined in relation to:

- the organisational structure or pyramid.
- whether the post relates directly to the promotion of race equality or provides support indirectly through the organisation.
- the four main constitutionally-defined functions (policy, community, awareness-raising, case work).
- the main public authority service-provider areas, such as education, training and youth, employment, housing and regeneration, criminal justice (including the police), and sometimes, health.
- the project management and delivery of specific time-limited project outcomes,

with staff given roles and titles related to the projects they are working on or the outcomes they are expected to deliver.

Organisational structure or pyramid

The following posts relate to positions in the line management structure.

Chief executive officer (CEO)

An REO's chief executive officer (CEO) was traditionally referred to as its director but, as more REOs become companies with boards of directors, to avoid confusion, the title 'director' for a paid employee is falling out of favour. CEOs have overall responsibility for delivering the work of the organisation and must have knowledge of, and skills in, managing people, projects, money and public relations.

CEO responsibilities

For the REO to be successful, its CEO will also have to keep abreast of current affairs and policy development and chart the organisation's strategic course. CEOs are responsible for servicing and advising the board and managing, directing, guiding and mentoring any other staff that the organisation may have at main grade or trainee level. Normally, CEOs have the difficult job of liaising with the heads of major bodies in the locality and steering the REO in a way that wins acceptance for its race equality promotional role.

Working for a local race equality organisation

Race equality officer

A race equality officer was traditionally seen as the main-grade officer in a REC. Indeed, many community relations councils or race equality councils had only two officers, consisting of the chief executive (or director) and the race equality officer (who had to take on those tasks remaining after the director had made a choice). Race equality officers took on a wide range of jobs, often including daily face-to-face contact with members of black and minority ethnic communities, and/or complainants of discrimination in employment, housing, education, police, and the courts. In the 1970s, this often involved explaining the provision of the Race Relations Act to people who were ignorant of its existence and provisions.

Professionalisation

Today, the job requires a greater knowledge of community needs or conditions in the neighbourhood and of the services provided locally by public authorities and private companies. Race equality officers' professionalism is judged on whether their intervention is supported by social scientific evidence and convincing arguments: the rhetoric of anger and indignation, however justified, will lead to external bodies closing their ranks against the REO.

Post supporting the race equality organisation

Administrator

An REO administrator oversees the organisation's administrative arrangements which, for a small organisation, can be a surprisingly wide-ranging and demanding task. More often than not, the administrator will also have responsibility for day-to-day financial control, ensuring income is received and expenditure is under control. The administrator is expected to run the office efficiently, which includes ensuring the information technology and other equipment, for example, photocopier, telephones, faxes, are working and all staff conform to office protocols in a concerted plan to deliver organisational outcomes. The administrator will line manage and support staff, including clerks and receptionists, and make sure that all people contacting the organisation in person, by telephone, post, or email, receive a professional and courteous service. Another time-consuming role involves arranging meetings and servicing the board and its sub-committees.

Multi-tasking

In small organisations, the administrator will have to double up as a personal assistant, secretary, or clerk to the chief executive, performing word-processing, communication, photocopying, and filing tasks as requested. In larger organisations, it may be possible to distinguish the functions of administrator from those of the finance officer, the personal assistant, clerk, secretary, and receptionist. In general, however, money for staffing is more likely to be allocated to race equality officer posts than to support work.

Finance officer

Financial management and control is a vital element of all voluntary and community sector organisations receiving grant aid, entering into service level agreements, tendering for contracts, and employing their own staff. It is self-evident that as annual budgets rise above the £100,000 mark, with funding coming in from different sources, each with its own conditions attached, the organisation may need to make use of full or part-time financial expertise. Currently, many small organisations will contract out their payroll function and this may be the answer to the growing demands for effective and transparent financial management. With most REOs registered as companies and charities, and being judged as worthy recipients of charitable funds on the basis of the proficiency of their financial management, however, further attention is likely to be paid to the specialist role of the REO finance officer.

Clerical, secretarial and reception

These functions are common to general office work in small organisations and show no sign of decline even in situations where the race equality officers are expected to undertake their own word processing and photocopying and to arrange meetings directly.

Continuing demand for clerical work

While websites and emails are essential to modern office practice, there are few signs that the demand for typed reports and printed publications is in decline. Indeed, there is an expectation that meetings will have formal agenda, supporting reports, and minutes approved and kept on file. In addition, clerical and secretarial staff have to deal with a torrent of electronic communication, and accompanying information storage and retrieval. Organisations are judged on the speed and quality of their responses and orderliness of their presentation.

Functionally-defined posts

Race equality policy officer

Larger REOs sometimes choose to develop a functionally-specialised staffing structure in terms of the modes of operation set out in their constitution (see CRE Revised Model constitution for RECs 1995). This identifies policy development within the public, private and voluntary sectors as a key function of REOs, although in practice most work of this nature has been targeted at the public sector.

Policy officer contact with public bodies

Race equality policy officers, therefore, usually have the brief of contacting and discussing with major public sector bodies dealing with housing, employment, education, health and criminal justice agencies, in particular the police, (but sometimes, local prisons and youth offending institutions), the effect of their policies and activities on race relations and ethnic communities.

REOs' role in consultation.

Officers' intervention will often be informed by maintaining contact with local communities and taking up individuals' complaints with the relevant body. In recent years, public authorities, increasingly aware of the importance of being responsive and sensitive to their users' demands, have put into place more systematic ways of gauging public opinion, and have sometimes involved REOs in this process, particularly when seeking to consult with ethnic minorities.

Community advocacy

Race equality workers have become useful sounding boards for some authorities and play a role in legitimising their approach to community provision. Nevertheless, it is difficult for a single officer to give useful expert advice across the full range of the very different kinds of public services. The role of the race equality policy officer is probably best conceived as an independent advocate or mediator between ethnic communities and complainants on the one hand, and large public authorities on the other. The post holder runs the danger of being perceived by communities as a paid apologist for the authority, or by the authorities as an outspoken, unreasonable propagandist for an extreme and unrepresentative section of public opinion.

Community development officer

Frequently funded by money intended to assist with urban regeneration, community development posts are usually aimed at engaging with excluded and hard-to-reach groups (consisting of disproportionately-large numbers of minority ethnic individuals) and persuading them to participate in socially-constructive or distractive activity. The work is often conceived in terms of targeted projects tackling social problems, for example, unemployed or disaffected young people, homelessness, street crime and vandalism, drug dealing and taking, poor school performance, illiteracy, or low participation in post-compulsory education. Sometimes, however, the projects have a positive focus, involving cross-cultural contact and collaboration, sport, recreation, dance, drama and the arts. With some ethnic communities, the emphasis is on supplementary education, the acquisition of a community language, or the celebration and renewal of cultural or religious traditions. The role of the community development officer may involve grant acquisition to embark on specific community projects, recruiting participants and volunteers in managing or working on projects, and evaluating their effectiveness.

Liaison with ethnic communities

The community development officer will be expected to liaise with different ethnic communities supporting the projects, and other similar workers employed by public authorities and voluntary organizations, e.g. youth and community workers, sports instructors, teachers, neighbourhood managers, housing officers, and the police. A more recent addition to the portfolio of REO community development work has been the task of building the capacity of black and minority ethnic groups in order to strengthen their contribution to advocacy, self-help, and service provision for their members. It should be clear from this brief account that community development work can be immensely varied.

Race equality case worker

Race equality case work involves providing information, advice and guidance on the law relating to racial discrimination in employment and the provision of goods and services. Race-equality officers engaged in this work undertake casework for those individuals who approach the REO for help with their complaint, and sometimes, where the complaint cannot be resolved in any other way, represent their clients at an Employment Tribunal or County Court.

Case management

This free legal advice service involving intensive case work with individuals can easily be overwhelmed by demand, particularly if stimulated by publicity. Officers need to have legal knowledge and skills, and experience in case work and representation. Case loads have to be consistently managed and maintained and cannot readily be transferred to other staff. Case workers are specialist workers and have to be dedicated to and prioritise their case work over other organisational obligations, making then an expensive and inflexible element in overall staff management arrangements. This has led in recent years to a decline in the number of REOs undertaking anything more than providing preliminary information and advice in this field and to a corresponding increase in the demand for a specialist referral agency to take on tribunal representation.

Support for victims of racial harassment.

Some REOs have extended the scope of individual case work and the case worker's role to supporting victims of racial harassment and violence under criminal law. This involves working in partnership with the police on race hate crime, liaising and supporting victims, and monitoring the kinds and locations of incidents to take preventive measures. Victims may incur racial harassment from neighbours, from strangers in the street and public places, from school students and in educational settings, at work, and in relation to the police.

(Public) education officer

The REO public education function has often been consolidated into a post of education officer, who is allocated the general role of publicising the organisation's functions to all its client groups: public authorities and funders, different ethnic communities, individual complainants and victims of discrimination, and the general public, through the press and media. This generic role often rests with the Chief Executive Officer. But this kind of function is capable of different interpretations.

Race awareness training

Responding to requests mostly from public authorities, some REOs have acquired race awareness training expertise and appointed training officers to market and provide appropriate training to public sector employees, including teachers, social workers, and the police, on race relations legislation and statutory requirements and different ethnic minority cultures. Others have collaborated with schools in enriching the curriculum with various multi-cultural history, music, creative writing, dance, drama, and arts projects.

Public awareness-raising

More recently, with the electoral success of racist far-right political parties, REOs have begun to focus more closely on raising public awareness about the myths surrounding immigrant numbers, crime, asylum seekers, refugees, and terrorists, and the dangers of extremism.

Public authority service-related posts

Service improvement roles

Staffing structuration based on REO functions has frequently been modified to reflect the field of operation of some of the main local service providers, who may have deliberately encourage this process by offering to fund or second staff into a post that more directly meets their perceived organisational priorities. Not surprisingly, REOs, short of funding, have responded by sprouting posts related to specific service-improvement areas, such as school liaison officer, youth (Connexions) officer, employment officer, housing officer, Asian women's health improvement officer, police liaison officer, community safety officer, and racial harassment victim support officer. The titles are self explanatory. In essence, they involve close collaboration with the relevant public authorities in order to eliminate institutional discrimination, implement race equality schemes, conduct community consultation, and deliver improved services.

Project management and delivery posts

Timed outcomes

Often funds for service improvement activities are time-limited, as are grants for urban regeneration and other projects. This, and the move to outcome-related funding, have resulted in REOs restructuring themselves and their work programmes into sets of time-bound projects, each with specific outcomes, milestones and outputs to deliver, their duration normally ranging from one to five years. This approach shifts the emphasis away from one of providing a continuous repetitive process as performed by, for example, a doctor, nurse, or teacher, or in the case of a REO, the chief executive officer, or complainant-aid case worker.

Reality of the continuation of time-limited projects

In reality, however, though devised for a limited duration to conform with the terms of the available funding, nearly all projects are based on analyses of continuing and unmet need which is unlikely to be suddenly satisfied on project termination. Nevertheless, most REOs are funded on a short-term basis and have had to take this into account when deciding their staffing structure and establishment. Typical time-limited posts of three years duration or less are: refugee integration worker, Asian women's health worker, and mentoring project manager.

Mentoring project manager

The mentoring project manager post serves as an example of project work. It involves creating a coordinating team to assemble a multi-racial list of one hundred suitable volunteer mentors who are then carefully matched on a one-to-one basis with one hundred mentors, nominated and selected on the basis of need by secondary schools or local agencies, or self-nominated, to form a supportive social learning relationship. This process is repeated for new mentees every year for three years. New mentors have to be trained and the whole process carefully recorded, monitored and evaluated. Collective social and recreational activities are interspersed with regular mentor-mentee meetings. This is a sophisticated exercise requiring high levels of professionalism and organisational expertise from all the project workers and especially the project manager. But at the end of the three-year funded project, there is no guarantee that this non-statutory activity will continue.

Ideal staffing structures

When a new REO comes into being - usually a race equality partnership - an opportunity presents itself to devise a staffing structure fit for purpose. While unlikely to be implemented in full because of budgetary constraints, one newly-devised structure is worth presenting as an indication of contemporary thinking on staffing arrangements.

While some of these posts have been described above and are already familiar, two of them are new.

Partnership development and community liaison officer

This officer has responsibility for developing community partnerships, developing local organisations, identifying and obtaining resources, and maintaining formal and informal links with partnerships and networks, including the LSP and CEN, and organisations in the public, private and voluntary sectors, in order to ensure the delivery of local race equality services.

Research officer

This post is established to provide research and development in support of the organisation's race equality promotion remit. It involves broad-based social scientific research and survey work to justify and support strategic objectives and to track user groups' changing needs and perceptions.

Working for a local race equality organisation

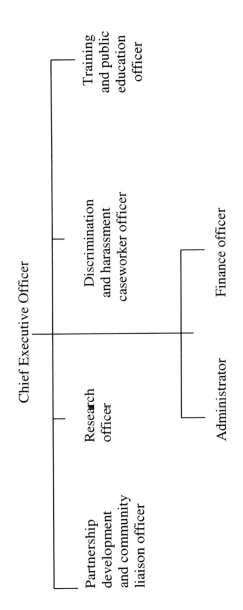

Chief Executive Officer

Partnership development and community liaison officer

Research officer

Discrimination and harassment caseworker officer

Training and public education officer

Administrator

Finance officer

Staff qualifications, experience, and training aspirations

Perspectives on race equality knowledge, values and skills.

Traditionally, two perspectives on the kind of knowledge, values and skills required to undertake race equality work have been apparent. These may be termed the intuitive experience approach and the rational expert approach, with the former gradually being displaced by the latter in the selection procedure for race equality officers.

Intuitive experience

The intuitive experience approach places great weight on the experience of ethnic minority status and of being on the receiving end of racism. Experience is regarded as an essential means of generating insight into race relations in order to take effective action against discrimination. Certainly, instances of discrimination need to be identified and highlighted.

Rational expert

The rational expert view is that in order to provide expert advice to public authorities seeking to improve their services to ethnic minorities, or to intervene successfully when race relations are in danger of breaking down, it is necessary to access the reservoir of objective knowledge, both theoretical and practical, on organisations and race relations. The job of promoting race equality is seen as requiring specialist knowledge and expertise. In this context, race equality work is not only about identifying and highlighting instances of discrimination, but of contributing to finding solutions.

Race equality officer qualifications

Recent surveys by REWM show that the vast majority of race equality officers are educated to at least first degree level, with more and more chief executive officers pursuing and obtaining qualifications at post-graduate level. Administrative staff have GCE, A level or NVQ 2 or 3 equivalent qualifications, and clerical and secretarial grades GCSE/NVQ. All current REO staff surveyed were educated to at least GCSE level. Staff have formal qualifications in many skill areas key to REO operations, the most frequently mentioned set out in the table below. Qualifications in clerical and administrative work are the most common, followed by qualifications in law, management, and race and ethnic relations.

Race equality staff experience

The table on page 103 shows the percentage of REOs where REOs claim to have staff with at least three years' experience in the key skills areas listed. Other areas of experience mentioned were immigration and international law, support for asylum seekers and refugees, translation and interpreting, equality training, mentoring, community development and empowerment activity, capacity-building, and mediation.

Percentage of REOs with staff having formal qualifications in key skill areas	
Areas of formal qualification	**% of REOs**
Clerical/administrative	56
Law degree	50
General management	44
Race and ethnic relations	31
Teaching/training	25
Youth and community work	25
Information technology/computing	25
Human resource management/development	19
Social research methods	19
Social work	19
Accounts, finance and banking	13
Marketing/public relations	6
Economic development/regeneration	0

Staff development and training

Nearly three quarters of REOs had established a budget for training staff members and volunteers, on average putting aside £4,000 per REO, but this figure ranged from £600 on the low side to £15,000 on the high, differences relating in part, but not entirely, to the size of the REO budget overall and the number of staff in post. REOs sometimes, but not always, distinguished between the budget set for training members of their executive, from the staff training budget, making it difficult to calculate a per capita staff training figure. On the basis of information supplied, REO annual per capita expenditure on staff development and training averaged £500.

Percentage of REOs having staff with at least three years' experience in listed skills areas	
Area	**Percentage**
Support for victims of racial harassment/violence	75
Education and school	69
Conflict resolution/medication	63
Public sector consultancy	56
Youth work	56
Employment tribunal representation	50
Legal advice and guidance	50
Police and crime prevention	50
Crime prevention	44
Legal casework	44
Health and social services	38
Consultancy in private sector	31
Housing	31
Interfaith work	31
Support for victims of domestic violence	25
Women's welfare	25
Working with young offenders	25
Disability rights work	19
Support for victims of drug abuse	19
Economic regeneration	13
Helping the aged or infirm	13
Support for victims of homophobic crime	6

Management training

Most respondents thought that REO staff would benefit from management training and would consider arranging for their release on a part-time basis, providing that practical problems of finding fees and suitable accredited training programmes could be solved. REOs also wanted a series of seminars to update their staff on development in the equalities field and were prepared to release staff to attend. Nearly all REOs had in place a staff appraisal policy and procedure, sometimes separate from, but often combined with, a staff development policy and procedure. A majority also had a staff development and training plan and programme. Many also had in place a training programme for members, officers, trainees and volunteers.

Critical success factors

Research into best practice in local race equality work, as well as into the reasons for the occasional total collapse of voluntary organisation in this field, has led REWM to identify various factors critical to the success of REOs. While the factors are not entirely discrete, the most vibrant organisations demonstrate to a large degree the following nine features.

- clear aims, objectives and priorities,
- strategic awareness and positioning,
- strong links with local communities,
- strong links with public authorities and other service providers,
- autonomy and independence,

- relevant, and reliable service provision,
- sustainability and developmental potential,
- competitive conditions to recruit and retain quality staff, and
- management expertise.

Clear aims, objectives and priorities

The successful REO has clear aims and objects, presents them clearly, translates them into a comprehensive wok programme commensurate to the staffing resources available, and establishes measurable outcomes which it pursues vigorously. Staff understand the vision, what is expected of them, and have an ambitious 'can-do' mentality. The organisation sets out precisely what it is about and what it is going to do, goes out and does it, and then makes sure it demonstrates publicly what it has succeeded in doing. The process of clarifying aims is particularly important in a context of rapidly changing circumstances. The external factors impacting on local equality work lead to the need for a constant revision of objectives and outcomes, and of the work programme devised to deliver them. The effects of the Commission for Equality and Human Rights, government prioritisation of community cohesion issues, public authorities' race equality duty, and the development and evolution of Local Strategic Partnerships and Local Area Agreements need constantly to be reviewed. Pronounced specialisation may be required in regard, for example, to race and faith work, community cohesion, and urban regeneration.

Strategic awareness and positioning

Equality organisations that fail to understand the power structures in which they operate, or the changing social climate, rapidly become isolated and irrelevant. Failure to sustain or generate increased economic resources impacts directly on the organisation's ability to deliver its objectives, but, in the long run, the inability to sustain or win political allies, or to enter into partnerships (or conversely, to avoid creating enemies) is equally damaging.

Avoiding a 'silo mentality'

If it is to have any relevance at all, an REO has to work closely with the public, private and voluntary sectors, and local communities themselves, to tackle social problems of health, crime, education, transport, housing and the local environment, each with its own significant (in)equality components An REO must avoid adopting an inward-looking 'silo mentality' and turn itself wholeheartedly outwards, working always at the interface with other agencies in the public, private, voluntary and community sector. In this respect, it has to become an 'inside-out' organisation, recognising that the only effective way of promoting and mainstreaming equality is in its relationship with others. Its effectiveness will be judged only on the way these relationships bring about changes in other social institutions.

Working for a local race equality organisation

Strong links with local communities

An REO must have close links with the communities it has been set up to serve. These communities of interest, or of residents, need to be sharply defined and targeted in line with the need for clarity of organisational vision. Some of the more vulnerable groups with which race equality organizations must engage are new and potential user groups. As might be expected, the groups with which established support agencies are least likely to relate to, meet with on a regular basis, or involve in the consultation process, are the ones least likely to receive equality of treatment in service provision or in other respects.

Links with potential client groups

The degree to which an equality organisation establishes and sustains supportive links with the communities it purports to serve is a central justification for its continued existence. An equality organisation that has little or no contact with groups, such as Gypsies and Travellers, asylum seekers or refuges, black and minority ethnic communities living in isolated rural areas, victims of Islamophobia, mixed-race people, or alienated and excluded white communities, yet claims the right to speak out on behalf of their interests, can have little credibility. REOs have the further task of improving relationships between communities that live separate or 'parallel lives' and which frequently exhibit their mistrust for one another (see Chapter Six). Bridge-building activities require the bridge builder to have firm foundations on either side of the divide.

Strong links with public authorities and other service providers

The government is committed to raising standards and improving services across the full range of public services. Success involves reaching all sections of the community, especially the most disadvantaged. Many public authorities have equality targets aimed at raising the standard of their services to particularly vulnerable groups. In addition, the Race Relations (Amendment) Act 2000 places a statutory duty on listed public authorities to promote race equality. Public authorities which have to produce race equality schemes are required to consult with the general public and service users on how best to ensure all racial groups are treated equally. Public authorities working in partnership are also expected to draw up a joint race equality strategy. The duty to promote race equality has now been extended to cover two other equality strands: gender and disability.

Autonomy and independence

Unlike large impersonal public authorities, voluntary sector bodies are regarded as being close to communities and in a strong position to articulate and aggregate local needs. The voluntary sector is thought to play a useful role in responding innovatively to emerging needs, in augmenting and plugging gaps in existing services, and in pressuring local government and public authorities to improve their practice. While being encouraged to work in partnership with local authorities, such as the police and local councils, and to seek funding from them, equality organisations should have sufficient freedom, autonomy and critical space to speak out against what they may judge to be unfairness in the operation of the public services.

Relevant and reliable service provision

Just as it should be clear about its aims and objects, and the groups it serves, an REO must be precise about the services it will provide and make them known to users and potential users. It has to be flexible in catering for the needs of its clients while, at the same time, maintaining its claim to specialist expertise. As a small organisation, it has to specialise and focus on what it is good at. Failure to satisfy expectation once generated, might jeopardise any further service level agreement and funding. There is a strong case for greater organisational specialisation in areas such as community cohesion projects and conflict resolution, or public education and awareness-raising. There is also the need to coordinate the various elements of equality work at local level and to incorporate them into a comprehensive local equality strategy or plan. In deciding on service range, the views of potential clients and user groups have to be taken into account. It is clear, for example, that local communities want complainant aid and victim support: services involving one-to-one casework and usually requiring expensive legal expertise. Funding for these kinds of service is not easy to obtain. For an REO to succeed, it is essential that it gets clear what services it wishes to provide and specialise in, and ensures that they remain relevant, reliable and accessible to all who need them. A scenario of 'mission drift' in search of funding has to be avoided if an REO is to succeed, not only on its own terms but, more critically, on those of others.

Sustainability and development potential

An REO has to be of a sufficient size and capacity to be able to undertake the jobs expected of it. The achievement of critical mass is essential to an equality body's success. Without a sufficient size it is unable to deliver services in sufficient quantity or quality. REO staff who are unable to specialise, or to hone their skills, rapidly relinquish any claim to be expert in their field. Overworked, they soon lose any creative get-up-and-go and resort to the kind of routine response that inevitably fails to bring about change. The key is the acquisition of income to pay for a complement of suitably-qualified staff. Paradoxically, as a result of the need for voluntary sector managers to persuade others to give their organisations money, the success of an REO's senior staff is no longer judged on the basis of knowledge and skill in the field, but on entrepreneurial skills, demonstrated by the speed with which the budget expands. A good manager is seen as one who is able to attract funding.

Competitive conditions to recruit and retain quality staff

Conditions of service in REOs have deteriorated in recent years. Nationally-agreed pay scales have been abandoned, and the CRE/REC pension scheme has been closed. If the staff of an REO are to provide quality services, they need attractive conditions, including opportunities for training and development.

This can only partly be achieved through higher rates of remuneration. Financial stability of the organisation, with permanent appointments, and some measure of career progression, would enhance staff prospects and, in the longer term, improve the quality of the service on offer. It is essential that an REO attracts staff who are sufficiently knowledgeable and skilled to provide advice and consultancy services that can be relied upon and respected. It needs to employ enough people to allow for specialisation. Increasingly, a requirement (particularly in this field) is for advice and decisions to be evidence-based, with the implication that some staff at least should have current knowledge of research techniques.

Management expertise

Management expertise is essential in any small organisation hoping to tap into a multiplicity of funding streams, to respond to the conditions imposed by different funding bodies, to elicit support from local communities, and to provide them with relevant high-quality services, as well as to mount successful projects and build a motivated team of staff. Indeed, precisely because REOs are often small organisations and comparatively politically and financially fragile, the senior staff member must have considerable management knowledge, skills and experience. Otherwise, organisations will fail, or at the very least, fail to live up to expectations. Having a good manager is a prerequisite for all successful organisational endeavour, and probably even more so in small voluntary sector service delivery agencies. Good highly-motivated and committed managers rarely emerge naturally, have often benefited from expensive management training, and come at a price.

Essential management skills

The essential management skills are entrepreneurship and financial management, human resource management (with sound knowledge of employment law), project management (projects and services have to be delivered on time to specification), and, specific to the job, diversity management. A knowledge of quality, contracts, and estates management does not come amiss, either. A manager will not be respected by a chair, executive committee, funders, public or private sector managers, politicians, or members of local communities, if these skills are not apparent on the job. Advice given to others on, for example, management of diversity, will not be appreciated if it is apparent that the advice giver is an incompetent manager.